F is for First State

A Delaware Alphabet

Written by Carol Crane and Illustrated by Elizabeth Traynor

I wish to gratefully acknowledge the following for invaluable contributions
to this book:

Beau Pendergraft; Mimi Traynor Pawliczek, photographer & historian; Cathy
Traynor; Shokie and Elizabeth Bragg; Jim Graham, photographer; Jan Durham of
Delaware State Parks Department; Tony Shahan and Greenbank Mills Associates;
Winterthur Museum & Gardens; and Jennifer Lundahl, Amy Lennex, and
Heather Hughes at Sleeping Bear Press for their patience & kindness.

—Elizabeth Traynor

Sleeping Bear Press™

310 North Main Street, Suite 300
Chelsea, MI 48118
www.sleepingbearpress.com

© 2005 Thomson Gale, a part of the Thomson Corporation.

Thomson, Star Logo and Sleeping Bear Press are trademarks
and Gale is a registered trademark used herein under license.

Printed and bound in China.

10 9 8 7 6 5 4 3 2

Library of Congress Cataloging-in-Publication Data

Crane, Carol, 1933-
F is for First State : a Delaware alphabet / written by Carol Crane ; illustrated by
Elizabeth Traynor.
p. cm.
ISBN 1-58536-154-2
1. Delaware—Juvenile literature. 2. English language—Alphabet—Juvenile literature.
I. Traynor, Elizabeth. II. Title.
F164.3.C73 2004
975.1—dc22   2004005264

Delaware is the First State and my editor
Denise Alekseev has been number one for me.
A huge thank you. Also, to my grandson Bryan, who traveled
with me throughout Delaware gathering information.

CAROL

~

To Alan Brown and Brian Scatasti,
without whom this book would not have been possible.
You are the next wave of talent,
and it has been a privilege to work with you.

And for Beau, so that you will remember what you knew first.

ELIZABETH

A is for American holly tree—
bright red berries and leaves of green.
As a symbol of our state,
is it something you have seen?

The American holly was adopted as Delaware's state tree on May 1, 1939. This tree can reach heights of 60 feet in Delaware and elsewhere up to 100 feet tall.

Since ancient times it has been used as a decorative symbol of the winter holiday season. Sussex County became known as the "Land of Holly," and Charles G. Jones Sr. became known as "Jones, the Holly Wreath Man." He saw an opportunity to market holly wreaths in the United States and in numerous foreign countries. This industry helped many rural families earn income during the 1930s.

Aa

B b

In 1939 the Blue Hen chicken was adopted as the official Delaware state bird. The history of the bird in the state goes back to the Revolutionary War. Delaware soldiers were known as the fighting Blue Hens. Storytellers compared the valiant soldiers to the bird through the soldier's military wear and bearing: blue coats, leather hats, high peaks adorned with red feather plumes, and their marching with great precision.

Over the years the Blue Hen chicken has been used as a symbol for newspapers, magazines, and political campaigns.

Fighting hearts and feathers of blue,
the Blue Hen Chicken is our B.
It is the official Delaware state bird,
a symbol of the brave and free.

What United States canal carries more tonnage of freight and goods than the Suez or Panama Canal? It is the Chesapeake and Delaware Canal! It took years to raise the money to dig the 14-mile lock canal. What began as a dream in the 1600s did not come true until the canal opened in 1829.

The canal connected Back Creek in Maryland to St. George's Meadow in Delaware. This shortcut eliminated a 300-mile, dangerous trip around the peninsula for farmers, merchants, and visitors. Cargo such as fruit and vegetables could arrive fresher. Passengers could travel between Baltimore and Philadelphia in less than a day. The Chesapeake and Delaware Canal continues to be a mode of transportation in Delaware.

There were few paved roads in the United States as the twentieth century began. In 1908 T. Coleman du Pont, a multimillionaire offered to build a modern highway the length of Delaware. It became the first divided highway in the world.

C will be the Chesapeake and Delaware Canal,
an old system of transportation.
A shortcut for business or pleasure,
a canal still in operation.

In the 1700s civic leader William Penn ordered that a square be laid out in Dover. It was called the Green. Here statesmen from Delaware gathered a Continental Regiment and voted to ratify the U.S. Constitution. Citizens celebrated the reading of the Declaration of Independence here. The Green has become the center of life for the county seat and state capital.

The Delaware State House was the first permanent capitol building in Dover and was located on the Green. It is now a museum. Here you can see a gilt sunflower ceiling medallion and a geometrical grand staircase.

In 1933 Legislative Hall, new the state capitol building, became the home of Delaware's 62 legislators. It also contains the chambers for the senate, the house of representatives, and is the governor's ceremonial office. The Delaware Liberty Bell is located on the lawn of Legislative Hall.

Dd

Laws and rules for all our citizens
are guaranteed and we agree,
they are made here at our state capital.
Dover, Delaware is our D.

Enchanted Woods is our E,
the home of woodland fairy folks.
A garden of magic and mystery,
charming all ages under the oaks.

Ee

This enchanted fairyland is on the grounds of Winterthur. Children and adults will find fantastic worlds to explore at the Enchanted Woods. Here imaginary friends have Story Stones, a Troll Bridge, S-s-s Serpentine Path, Water Edge Fairie Cottage, an Acorn Tearoom, and many other creative make-believe places where children and adults can enjoy the beauty and playfulness of Oak Hill.

The historic Winterthur estate, located just outside Wilmington, was home to Henry Francis du Pont. Du Pont was an antique collector who established the Winterthur Museum, Garden, and Library. The Winterthur Museum is home to china dinnerware that was made for George Washington.

F is for the First State—
first to confirm our Constitution.
F is also for our Flag,
with honored colors in our nation.

John Dickinson was a delegate from Delaware at the Constitutional Convention in 1787. He had written letters and articles opposing British rule and defending the rights of Americans. He presided over the convention. When the new Constitution was submitted to the states for ratification, Delaware was the first of the 13 original states to ratify the Constitution of the United States. The unanimous ratification took place in Dover and Delaware became "The First State" of the new federal union. As the first state to ratify the Constitution, Delaware was given the honor to be in the lead position in national events such as parades and presidential inaugurations.

The Delaware Flag was adopted as the state flag on July 24, 1913. The colors of the flag represent and honor those colors in the uniform of General George Washington.

Below the diamond are the words "December 7, 1787,"–the date Delaware ratified the Constitution. Inside the diamond, Delaware pays tribute to the Revolutionary War soldiers, and also shows the importance of the farmer, the ox, the wheat sheaf, corn, a ship, and water. The words Liberty and Independence appear on a banner near the bottom of the diamond.

LIBERTY AND INDEPENDENCE

DECEMBER 7, 1787

Ff

Greenbank Mill is our **G**
where in 1784
Oliver Evans demonstrated a flour mill
that eased a backbreaking chore.

G g

The 300-year-old Greenbank Mill is still in operation today.

Inventor Oliver Evans had an idea for a high-pressure steam engine that would help mill wheat into flour with less work. An additional plus would be cleaner flour. Mr. Evans received one of the first three patents ever granted by the U.S. Patent Office.

Robert Philips, a Quaker, purchased Greenbank Mill on Red Clay Creek. Water flowing from the creek provided power for a mill. Together, these two men set up a new system of industrialization. After seeing that Mr. Evans' system worked, other millers installed it in their mills.

H h

H is for the Horseshoe Crab—
it has two sets of eyes.
The official marine animal of our state,
easy to recognize.

The horseshoe crab has survived for millions of years. Delaware recognized it as our state marine animal in 2002.

It gets the name "horseshoe" from the U-shape of its shell. It has no trouble hiding in the muddy or sandy beach bottoms because its shell is the same color. Its two eyes are on the top of its shell. This allows the crab to be able to see in all directions and detect movement. Another set of eyes is located on each side of a small spine, near the front of the shell. The horseshoe crab has seven pairs of legs to move around with and push food into its mouth.

In 1996 *Belemnite* was named the official fossil of Delaware. It is a squid with a conical shell. The fossil can be found along the banks of the Chesapeake and Delaware Canal, in northern Delaware.

In the 1700s a ship ran aground on a river shoal with a cargo of peas. The peas sprouted and grew in the sandy soil and legend has it that is how Pea Patch Island got its name. Located on the Delaware River, Fort Delaware was built there to guard river access to Wilmington, New Castle, and Philadelphia. The 32-foot-high walls are built of solid granite blocks and more than 25 million bricks. A moat surrounds the fort and can be crossed by a drawbridge.

Through the years the fort reached a capacity of 6,000 troops, but was slowly dismantled until the state of Delaware took it over in 1949. In 1950 a dedicated group organized the Fort Delaware Society and worked with the Department of Natural Resources and Environmental Control toward the care and development of Fort Delaware State Park. A nature preserve is now located there. Herons, egrets, and ibises lay their eggs and raise their young in this protected environment.

Today you can also travel back in time and see how people lived and worked in Fort Delaware in 1863.

I is for a very important Island,
Pea Patch by name.
It is also the location of Fort Delaware,
claiming great fame.

Ii

J is for the Jewels of the diamond state,
our 14 state nature parks—
rolling hills and sandy beaches,
Delaware's golden trademarks.

J j

Thomas Jefferson compared Delaware to a diamond, small but very valuable. He said, "Delaware is a jewel among states due to its strategic location on the Eastern seaboard."

Delaware has become a nature playground for its own families as well as many people in the major cities of the mid-Atlantic region. The 14 state park "jewels" include Bellevue, Brandywine Creek, Cape Henlopen, Delaware Seashore, Fenwick Island, Fort Delaware, Fort duPont, Fox Point, Holts Landing, Killens Pond, Lums Pond, Trap Pond, White Clay Creek, and Wilmington State Park, which includes the Brandywine Zoo.

Every year festivals are held at our state parks and kids have fun sailing kites or learning about the history of our state.

K k

K is for *Kalmar Nyckel*,
Delaware's famous tall ship.
It sailed bringing settlers,
four times it made a round trip.

The *Kalmar Nyckel* landed in the New World on the banks of the Christina River, which is a tributary of the mighty Delaware River. The site became known as "The Rocks." The settlers onboard had sailed from Sweden with 25 men. Some of the crew came from Sweden, others from Finland, Holland, and Germany. One man was a black freedman from the Caribbean, Anthoni, called the Black Swede. People onboard spoke different languages and had different cultures, but worked together to build a fort and settle in this new land.

The *Kalmar Nyckel* sailed back to Europe and two years later returned with women and children.

Today the ship has been recreated as an Ambassador of Good Will. The ship is a training vessel and a model of life from 350 years ago.

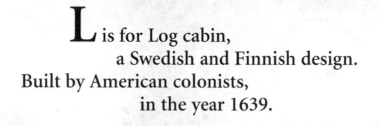

L is for Log cabin,
      a Swedish and Finnish design.
Built by American colonists,
      in the year 1639.

When the Swedish and Finnish colonists settled in what is now called Fort Christina, at Wilmington, Delaware, they brought with them the design of a cabin they had used in their native countries, the one-room log cabin. Later, as pioneers moved west, they built these cabins throughout America.

The floors were made of stones, a perfect foundation for the logs to rest on. The settlers used white oak logs, stacking them and placing them into walls using no nails or pegs. Spaces between the logs were filled with a mixture of mud, grass, and the top part of oats. Finally, the cabin featured a fireplace for cooking and keeping warm. Log cabins were strong and solid shelters for early settlers.

M is for the Mason-Dixon line,
two men hired to survey.
In the 1700s they marked a boundary
still recognized today.

Two English surveyors, Charles Mason and Jeremiah Dixon, were commissioned by the King of England to come to America and resolve a long-standing land dispute between the Calvert family and the Penn family.

Mason and Dixon arrived in Philadelphia and began to survey the Delmarva Peninsula. Delmarva made up the area that is now Delaware, Maryland, and Virginia.

They worked four years marking the border between two colonies, Maryland and Pennsylvania.

A crown stone was placed every five miles. The crown stone had the coat of arms for the Penns on one side and the coat of arms for the Calverts on the other side. Many of these stones are still standing today.

Many Americans use the Mason-Dixon line as a dividing line between the Northern and Southern states of the United States.

The Native Americans were the original inhabitants of Delaware. The Lenni-Lanape tribe, or Delaware Indians, lived in the northern regions, while the Nanticoke lived in the southwest.

The Delaware Indians and the state were both named after the Delaware River. The Delaware's oval-shaped houses were made from trees covered with bark.

The Nanticoke were known as the People of the Tidewater. They were experts with the canoe and knew how to navigate the water around the Delaware River and Bay.

Today both Native American tribes live in a modernized world. However, many still honor the old ways and traditions. Each September a festive powwow is held in Delaware where Nanticoke Indians gather to share their stories of pride, spirit, and determination.

N
n

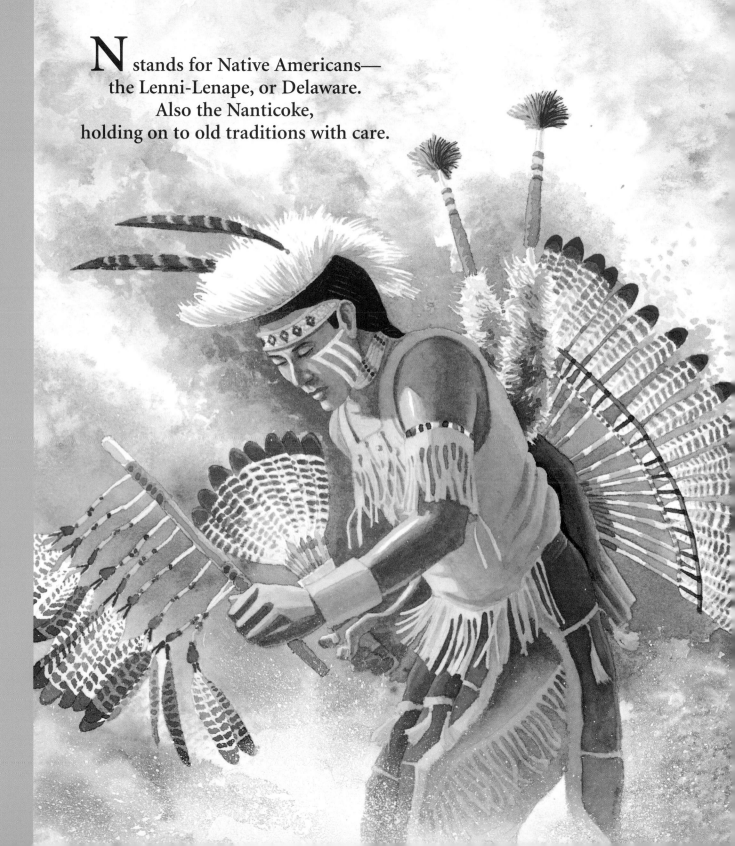

N stands for Native Americans—
the Lenni-Lenape, or Delaware.
Also the Nanticoke,
holding on to old traditions with care.

When the Swedes first settled in America in 1638 they built Fort Christina in Wilmington, naming it after the young queen of Sweden. On the next rise of ground they placed the burying ground. In 1698 the church was built over some of the early graves. In church records it shows that there are graves under the church walls. It is recognized as the nation's oldest church building still standing as originally built.

The pulpit, made of black walnut, is the oldest known pulpit in the United States. The pews, or bench seats, were enclosed to keep worshippers warm. They brought heated rocks to put their feet on during the service.

Old Swedes Church still has regular worship services every Sunday.

O is for Old Swedes Church,
built by Swedish pioneers.
Oldest pulpit, and inside, graves—
a church for 300 years.

The Spanish brought the peach to the New World,
a very bountiful fruit tree.
The blooms became our state flower,
so Peach blossom is our **P**.

In the 1680s William Penn arrived in Pennsylvania and Delaware and found that Native Americans were growing peaches. The climate and growing season were just right to make peaches become very plentiful throughout the state. In 1875, Delaware's peak year of peach production, 8.7 millions of baskets of peaches made their way to market.

Poems and songs were written about Delaware's sweet peaches. The peach blossom became the state flower in 1895 in honor of the peach's importance to Delaware's agriculture and economy.

P is also for Howard Pyle, a famous artist from Wilmington whose *Book of Pirates* offered visions of life on the high seas. Pyle is considered the Father of Illustration and also illustrated books such as *The Merry Adventures of Robin Hood, The Story of King Arthur and His Knights,* and many more. He had many famous students, including the artist N.C. Wyeth.

Caesar Rodney was born near Dover, Delaware in 1728 and died in Dover in 1784. During his lifetime he was a judge, governor, soldier, and patriot.

In July 1776, two delegates were in a dispute in Philadelphia as to whether they should break away and become independent from England or stay loyal to the king of England. Caesar Rodney rode his horse 80 miles and arrived just as the voting session was to begin. His famous statement: "As I believe the voice of my constituents and all sensible and honest men is in favor of independence, my judgment concurs with them: I vote for independence." He broke the tie between the delegates as a signer of the Declaration of Independence.

Delaware's state quarter was the first in the 50 State Quarters® Program, minted in 1999.

In 1934, a statue of Caesar Rodney was chosen to represent Delaware in Statuary Hall in Washington D.C.

Q stands for the 1999 state Quarter,
        Caesar Rodney riding to cast his vote.
"I vote for independence,"
        was this famous American statesman's quote.

R is for the National Wildlife Refuge,
known as Bombay Hook.
So many waterfowl to record
in my bird notebook.

Bombay Hook National Wildlife Refuge was established in 1937. It is home to many migrating birds and wintering ducks and geese. This is part of the Atlantic Flyway. From October through November, approximately 150,000 ducks and geese stop at the refuge. The area includes thousands of acres of tidal salt marshes, swamps, and freshwater pools.

The history of this area goes back to the 1600s. The Native Americans called it *Canaresse*, meaning "shaggy bushes." The Dutch name *Bompies Hoeck* means "little tree point." Bombay Hook is the habitat for wood ducks, pintail ducks, herons, egrets, glossy ibises, and many more beautiful birds, including the bald eagle. Some mammals include white-tailed deer, muskrat, red fox, and beaver.

There are observation towers where you can take pictures. On quiet nature trails you can walk and make notes in a special nature journal about the different species you see.

Rr

S s

S stands for Stars.
Who would think to count them?
Annie Jump Cannon did just that,
each sparkly nighttime gem.

As a little girl, Annie Jump Cannon loved to stargaze from her roof in Dover, Delaware. Her mother taught her about the constellations. When she went to college she studied the science of stars, called astronomy. She wanted to learn about them and came up with a scheme to catalog their names.

She used the phrase "Oh! Be A Fine Girl—Kiss Me," the letters being O B A F G K M. She classified them starting with "O" stars, which are the bluest and hottest, down to the coolest red stars, known as "M" stars. The stars at the beginning of the sequence are called "early-type" stars and at the end, "late-type" stars. The colors range from white to yellow to orange. Different temperatures of the stars cause the distinction.

Her eye for telling the difference between stars led her to catalog nearly 400,000 different ones. This catalog is still used today. So when you go out at night and look up at the stars, just think of Annie Jump Cannon, who named them!

Three butterflies were chosen by Delaware students and sent for approval to the state legislature as a possible state butterfly. The tiger swallowtail butterfly was declared the official state butterfly in 1999.

The tiger swallowtail is a large winged butterfly, yellow in color with black stripes. It can be found throughout the state. How many times have you seen this beautiful butterfly? Have you looked in your garden, along riverbanks, streams, or in the woods?

In 1974 a second grade class from Milford, Delaware, petitioned to have the ladybug named as Delaware's state insect. It took many months of campaigning, but the legislature finally approved the ladybug as the state insect in 1974.

Tiger swallowtail butterfly is our T.
Children were asked to decide:
"Which butterfly shall win the vote?"
"Tiger swallowtail," they replied.

Tt

U stands for Underground Railroad,
where slaves found a friend indeed.
His name was Thomas Garrett,
a Quaker helping many in need.

Thomas Garrett was an abolitionist. An abolitionist did not believe in slavery. Garrett worked for years hiding, feeding, and clothing slaves who were escaping north to freedom. Even though he was threatened many times and lost all of his money, he secretly worked as a "station-master" of the Underground Railroad.

Thomas Garrett was also a Quaker, and through his faith he helped more than 2,000 slaves reach freedom. He was called "Our Moses" by slaves in Wilmington and was carried on their shoulders through the streets.

A marker has been erected in Wilmington honoring his humanitarism.

U u

Listening to old-time music,
    sitting on Grandpa's knee,
see the record go 'round and 'round—
    Victrola is our V.

In the early 1900s E.R. Johnson, an inventor and businessman, made it possible for people to enjoy music in their homes. He invented the "talking machine" that played round cylinder discs, then round flat records. A needle was applied to the record, and as it turned around and around, music came out of a large horn. "Nipper," the dog with his head cocked, listening at the horn of an old-time record player, is a famous logo of the Victor Talking Machine Company. Later, speakers were used in wooden cabinets to amplify the music.

Families would gather around the talking machine, singing and dancing to the music. Someone would have to turn the handle when the music slowed down.

A collection of thousands of records and old-time talking machines can be seen in a museum in Dover, Delaware, the hometown of Mr. Johnson.

A gateway to business and research,
museums for everyone.
W History, rivers, and gardens,
is our proud Wilmington.

Wilmington grew on the banks of two rivers, the Brandywine and the Christina. The people of Wilmington have worked together to make this city great for over 350 years.

Wilmington has been called the "Corporate Capital" as many banks and big businesses have moved to the state to take advantage of the business-friendly tax laws.

National Landmarks have given all citizens a chance to step back in time and see mansions and gardens as they were in the seventeenth century. The Delaware History Museum, Hagley Museum, and Willingtown Square, where six restored eighteenth century houses are located, show us the various ways homes were lived in years ago.

Delaware has three counties: New Castle in the north, Kent County in central Delaware, and Sussex in southern Delaware.

Northern Delaware serves as the entrance to the Brandywine Valley. Here you will see rolling hills and rich farmlands. In Kent County you will find the capital city, Dover. In Sussex County you will find waterways with sandy beaches and fun places to shop.

Delaware's state seal represents parts of each county's seal. The wheat sheaf, from the Sussex County seal, illustrates agriculture. New Castle County's ship building industry is shown by the ship and represents Delaware's coastal industry. Corn is taken from the Kent County seal, also showing agriculture in the state.

Delaware is 2,044 square miles, 96 miles in length, and 39 miles wide. In size, it ranks 49th in the United States.

X

NEW CASTLE

Del. River

NEW JERSEY

GREAT SEAL OF THE STATE OF DELAWARE

LIBERTY AND INDEPENDENCE

·1793·1847·1907·

Delaware Bay

MARYLAND

KENT

SUSSEX

Delaware has three counties,
I know it is not a lot.
In one you'll find Dover.
The letter X marks the spot.

Yy

Y is for steel Yachts,
sailing vessels low and sleek.
The pride of Wilmington,
America's Cup they did seek.

Over 100 years ago an iron yacht was built to compete in the America's Cup race. The *Mischief* was built in Wilmington, Delaware. It was also called the "Iron Pot," because at that time, yachts were made of mostly wood. It was 61 feet long.

The people of Wilmington waited anxiously to hear how their boat was doing in the 1881 America's Cup race. Was she ahead or lagging behind? When it was announced that *Mischief* had won the famous sailing race, those that had built the iron vessel were very proud. The *Mischief* had made history.

The Dutch sent explorers to America to open up the Dutch West India Company in 1621. They believed whales were in the area, and 28 men were sent to hunt whales, grow tobacco, and trade with the Native Americans.

In 1931 the Zwaanendael Museum was built in Lewes to commemorate the 300th anniversary of the first European settlement in Delaware. The museum is the design of the city hall in Hoorn, the Netherlands. It has Dutch-style architecture, which looks like steps with gables. It has a baked clay tile roof. The front of the building is decorated with sandstone carvings and on the very top is a statue of Captain David Pietersen DeVries who led the expedition to the New World.

The H.M.S. *DeBraak*, a small powerful vessel called a brig, was hit by a violent squall and sank off the Delaware coast in 1798. The brig went down in 80 feet of water. Two hundred years later archaeological items were recovered and are on display at the museum. Through its exhibits you learn about the 1767 Cape Henlopen Lighthouse, the Bombardment of Lewes during the War of 1812, and many other stories of southeastern Sussex County's maritime history.

Found are historic treasures, including
H.M.S. *DeBraak* from the deep sea.
In Dutch it's called "Valley of Swans,"
Zwaanendael Museum is our Z.

Zz

First State Questions

1. In Delmar is the Delmarva Peninsula's museum of railroad artifacts. What is the "highball signal"?

2. The only Revolutionary battle on Delaware soil was fought at what bridge?

3. Who became the first African American to be ordained an Episcopal Priest?

4. Emily P. Bissell designed the first stamp for people to buy and help stamp out what disease?

5. Who was Samuel Burris?

6. What is the official state beverage of Delaware?

7. What English navigator discovered Delaware River and Bay for the Dutch East English Company?

8. Fort Christina was named for what queen?

9. Where can you see over one million-bird eggs, a large collection of seashells and an international collection of mammals?

10. Where was Delaware's colonial capital on the Delaware River?

11. What is the Delaware Diamond?

12. What were around long before dinosaurs and marine reptiles?

13. What is the Tran peninsular line?

14. What is a cupola?

15. Christmas in the Hendrickson House was very special. Where did the Christmas tree and decorations come from?

16. What is called the "Nation's Summer Capital"?

17. What is a weakfish?

18. During World War II, Observation Towers were placed along Lewes Beaches as a reminder of what?

19. Who was called the "Penman of the American Revolution."

20. What is the first town in the First State?

1. Signals of this type were used on early railroads to control train movements. When the track was clear, the station agent would hoist the ball, permitting the train to proceed.

2. Cooch's Bridge

3. Absalom Jones, a former slave, who bought his freedom and established the Free African Society in 1787.

4. Tuberculosis. She started the first Christmas Seal stamp.

5. A native of Delaware, he helped many slaves escape through the Underground Railroad. He was caught and imprisoned, but a friend bought him at a slave auction so he could escape.

6. Milk was made the state beverage in 1983.

7. Henry Hudson was hoping to find a faster route to India.

8. Fort Christina was named for the young queen of Sweden.

9. The Delaware Museum of Natural History where you can also see a living Australian barrier reef.

10. Old New Castle

11. It is the designated state star of Delaware, the first star on the International Star Register ever to be registered as an American State.

12. Belemnites, the state fossil of Delaware.

13. It is the line established as the east-west boundary between Pennsylvania and the three lower counties, (now Delaware)

14. Cupolas are small rounded structures found on top of a roof. Cupolas are found on the top of the New Castle Court House built in 1782 and Legislative Hall in Dover serving Delaware since 1933.

15. In the 1800's, Christmas tree decorations were made fresh each year and hung on a freshly cut tree. This was an era before electric lights and plastic trees.

16. Rehoboth Beach-Dewey Beach is just two hours from Washington D.C. on the Atlantic Ocean and many visitors from the Washington area enjoy the sun, sand and great ocean crabbing and shellfish eating. Rehoboth was a Methodist camp meeting site in the 1800's and means "room for all".

17. The Weakfish or Sea trout was adopted as Delaware's state fish.

18. During World War II, it was important to look out for sub-marines or other ships that may try to invade the United States. These cement towers are still in place as a reminder of the importance of Delaware's strategic coastal waters.

19. John Dickinson

20. 32 Dutch settlers stepped ashore in 1631, on the shores of Lewes. They proclaimed the area "Valley of the Swans".

Carol Crane

As a historian, Carol loves looking through the kaleidoscope of the past and has taken many delightful journeys through Delaware. She loves to imagine her Swedish ancestors coming to this country on the *Kalmar Nyckel*, building log cabins, or starting the first Swedish church in Wilmington. Galloping through the countryside envisioning Caesar Rodney's ride, Carol Crane finds Delaware very deserving of its motto, the First State.

Carol lives with her husband Conrad in North Carolina. Traveling in their van to speak at education conferences across the nation, with camera, journal, and pen in hand, she loves learning everything she can about this great country.

Elizabeth Traynor

Elizabeth Traynor was the only child in her kindergarten class who knew that blue + yellow = green. She decided to be an illustrator when she was 15 years old, while taking art classes at the Delaware Art Museum. She received her BFA in illustration from Rhode Island School of Design and has been an illustrator ever since. Her work can be seen throughout the country, from books, newspapers and magazines, to ads and packaging. She also teaches illustration, passing her love and knowledge of the field onto the next generation of artists.

Elizabeth lives with her son Beau a budding artist himself, and their cat Junebug. She divides her time between the Delaware Valley and California. Her work can be seen at theispot.com/artist/traynor or at elizabethtraynor.com.